YOUTUBE RESEARCH

Growth Course Guide

Make Youtube Money with Channel Domination
How To Turn Youtube Dummies into Youtube Niche Ninjas
Yotube Algorithm Growth Hacking Seo Marketing Secrets & Tips

BY: DANIEL MARTIN
THEGREENCABBY & PASSIVECASHSTACKER

Youtube
Research
Growth Course
Guide

Make Youtube Money with Channel Domination

How To Turn Youtube Dummies into Youtube Niche Ninjas

Youtube Algorithm Growth Hacking Seo Marketing Secrets & Tips

BY: DANIEL MARTIN

Table of Contents

Copyright, Disclaimers and Legal Gobldygoop.

indication of your future success or results. Monetary and income results are based on many factors. We have no way of knowing how well you will do, as we do not know you, your background, your work ethic, or your business skills or practices. Therefore, we do not guarantee or imply that you will get rich, that you will do as well, or make any money at all. There is no assurance you'll do as well. If you rely upon our figures; you must accept the risk of not doing as well.

IF YOU DON'T TAKE MASSIVE AMOUNTS OF ACTION, YOU WILL ACCOMPLISH NOTHING! SO GET OUT THERE AND MAKE IT HAPPEN, ONE VIDEO AT A TIME!

PLEASE READ ENTIRE DOCUMENT BEFORE YOU IMPLEMENT ANY OF THE ACTIONS

There are a few types of fundamentals in this document. <u>**All of them work,**</u> yet some can get you into deep water with youtube and google. If there are no markings next to the **BOLD Heading,** then the fundamental is for everyone. If there is (Grey Hat Strategy) next to the **Bold Heading** some may not agree with the strategy but you should be ok in the eyes of youtube and google. If there is (Black Hat Strategy) next to the **Bold Heading** some may not agree with the strategy and you could get into Hot Water with youtube and google, including account strikes or even getting your account banned. Though (Black Hat Strategies) are Very effective, you need to weigh the Pro's and Con's of the possible outcomes. Many people utilize the black hat strategies when doing affiliate marketing or driving traffic to a website or other property. NOW IT IS TIME TO HAVE SOME FUN!

Greetings. Thanks for joining me today as you embark on your road to dominating youtube one video and playlist at a time.

I HAVE ASSEMBLED A LOT OF YOUTUBE AND VIDEO RELATED BONUSES AS A SPECIAL THANK YOU FOR YOUR SUPPORT & BOOK PURCHASE. THE LINK TO THIS MASSIVE YOUTUBE VIDEO BONUS IS ON THE LAST PAGE OF THIS BOOK YOU CAN

ACCESS IT HERE

I am Daniel Martin THEGREENCABBY THEGREENPREPPER PASSIVECASHSTACKER and many other channel aliases. For 12+ Years I have gotten a monthly check from YT monetization with my main Channel THEGREENCABBY and 9 other authority channels, all while managing over 300 others. I have worn the hat of Youtube Creator, Influencer, YT Network Administrator, Analytics & SEO Industry buff and a lover of all things learning and teaching. I have personally reviewed over 500 products and created 5,000+  videos. While youtubing, I have accumulated over 75,000 Subscribers 10.5 MILLION VIEWS in 222 countries & average 520,000 watch minutes per month on my flagship channel! I specialize in all things Youtube & we are here to help you *Learn and Grow* while doing what you love!! If you lay the foundation of fundamentals for your channel and follow the tips, tricks and hacks that we have learned in the last 12 years, you can do anything you like in the realm of youtube.

Let me help show you how to start optimizing your You Tube channel and give you valuable and constructive advice so that you can reach out to a bigger audience. Gaining more subscribers, watch time and dollar bills. **I won't add a lot of fluff or unnecessary words** just to keep you reading. I get down to the facts and techniques that I have learned and implemented. Let's start taking some massive action....... RIGHT NOW!

Most important TOPICS to Dominate any Youtube Niche

1) social profiles

2) tags, titles, descriptions, thumbnails

3) click through rate and watch time

4) quality and consistent content uploads

5) automation of tasks

There are 4 Video Ranking Factors to consider when you are trying to dominate any youtube keyword.

AFTER YOU GET DOWN THE BASICS - Collaborations can be found at

https://channelpages.com/ Choose your category

http://yttalk.com/forums/collaborations-meet-ups.42/

WE ARE ABOUT TO GET DOWN TO BUILDING UP CHANNEL SEO & AUTHORITY!

VIDEO SEO
Tags/Hashtags
Titles/Descriptions
Closed Captions
Translations

CLICK THROUGH INTERACTIONS
Watchtime/Likes
Comments/Hearts
Shares/Subscribes

SYNDICATION
Backlinks/Embeds

CHANNEL SEO & AUTHORITY
Tags/About
Playlists
Niche Videos

Youtube Video

4 Video Ranking Factors

Channel Home Section:

Setup playlist sections UP TO 10 so new viewers can quickly get to your NICHE content like BUSINESS ENGLISH, ENGLISH POETRY, BEST ENGLISH GRAMMAR also have a section for MOST POPULAR UPLOADS. I would add one section for each playlist and organize them by most popular content as said by channel analytics.

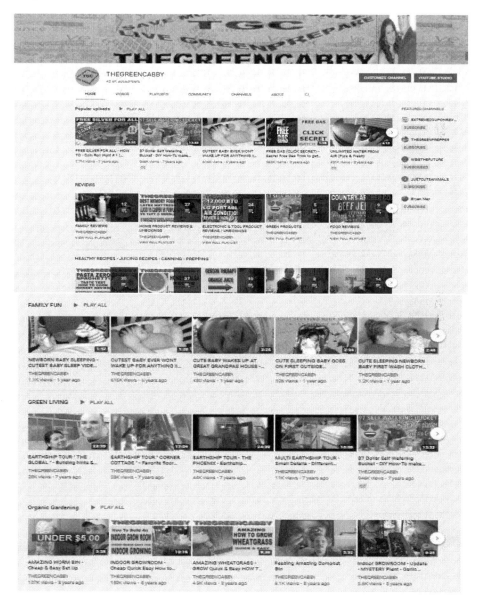

SUSTAINABILITY

AQUAPONICS MADE EASY & CHEAP
THEGREENCABBY -

Cheap & Easy $40 AQUAPONICS / LARGE SCALE DIY How-To Barrelponics Aquaponic Set Up - 16:52
AQUPONICS MEDIA GUARD - Cheap & Easy $40 AQUAPONICS / LARGE SCALE - 6:07
VIEW FULL PLAYLIST (12 VIDEOS)

BIODIESEL HOW-TO DIY LARGE SCALE
THEGREENCABBY -

HOW TO MAKE BIODIESEL LARGE SCALE AT HOME - BIOFUEL - METHANOL DISTILLATION - GL... - 2:34
NO MESS!: HOW TO FILTER LARGE AMOUNTS OF WVO USED VEGETABLE OIL FOR BIODIESEL S... - 2:40
VIEW FULL PLAYLIST (3 VIDEOS)

DIY CHICKENS
THEGREENCABBY -

EASY DIY CHICKEN COOP MANSION $50 - Poultry Farming Hen House for Raising Chickens - 1:52
HOW TO MAKE AN AUTOMATIC CHICKEN FEEDER - HOW TO FEED CHICKENS BULK CHICKEN F... - 1:05
VIEW FULL PLAYLIST (4 VIDEOS)

HOUSEHOLD HOW TO PROJECTS
THEGREENCABBY -

HOW TO MAKE OLAY BODYWASH - HOMEMADE FROM SCRATCH- BODY WASH & SHOWER GE... - 10:01
How To Make 5 Minute INSECT REPELLENT SOAP - MOSQUITO REPELLENT SOAP - ESSENTIA... - 12:08
VIEW FULL PLAYLIST (30 VIDEOS)

SHOW MORE

MAKE MONEY · EBAY · GARAGE SALES · COIN ROLL HUNTING

EBAY TIPS & TRICKS	MAKE $500 A DAY w/ GARAGE SALES & STOCKPILE SALES	COIN ROLL HUNTING SUCCESS	CONTROVERSIAL REAL ESTATE
THEGREENCABBY	THEGREENCABBY	THEGREENCABBY	THEGREENCABBY
VIEW FULL PLAYLIST	VIEW FULL PLAYLIST	VIEW FULL PLAYLIST	VIEW FULL PLAYLIST

Uploads   ▶ PLAY ALL

GEGOUCEY TWIN HYBRID MATTRESS UNBOXING -...	KISS MY KETO GUMMIES TASTE TEST REVIEW...	KISS MY KETO BARS TASTE TEST REVIEW- KETO FAT...	SERENELIFE TREADMILL UNBOXING ASSEMBLY...	12' WONEW SELFIE RING LIGHT WITH TRIPOD STAN...
140 views · 1 month ago	117 views · 2 months ago	182 views · 2 months ago	1.1K views · 2 months ago	2.5K views · 3 months ago
CC	CC	CC		

Past live streams   ▶ PLAY ALL

WAR OF THE SPARK PRERELEASE 58 BOOSTER...	How To Install Tubebuddy on Mozilla FIREFOX - Install...	How To Install Tubebuddy on Google Chrome - Install Tub...
106 views ·	362 views ·	335 views ·
Streamed 1 year ago	Streamed 1 year ago	Streamed 1 year ago

Channel Tags:

SUPER IMPORTANT!! You need to populate your channel tags with up to 500 characters. Max This Out! This is how youtube and google know what will be on your channel. VERY IMPORTANT! Use as many keywords as you can think of that describes what content you release. Many ways to find tags and keywords explained a little later.

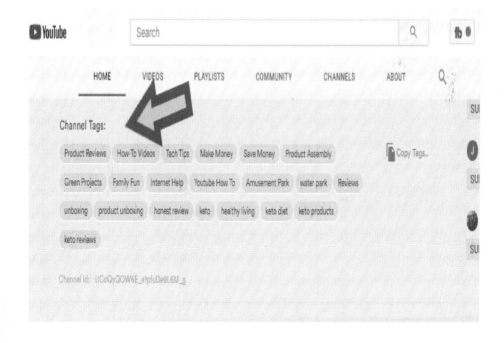

Youtube Home Page Outbound Links:

Add all social links on your channel banner to create more interaction and loyalty. Place social links to twitter facebook and website to grow channel authority, and social backlink traffic.

Channel About Section:

You will want to max out the channel ABOUT section with keyword rich sentences on what your channel is about. These keywords will help google and youtube decide on who to send to your channel. They will both read this information with their algorithm and will decide what type of traffic to send to you - include as many keywords related to channel niche and variations of those keywords as you can so they can send you that type of traffic and viewership.

Always include business contact email in the about section for reviews, collaborations or fan mail. This will help your growth and open up many possibilities.

Include your social links here to garner more interaction, channel growth and open subscriber communication.: Facebook, Twitter, Website

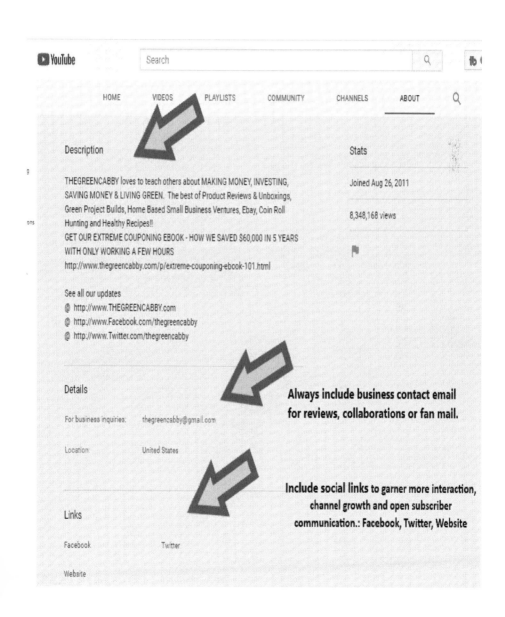

Playlists:

Every single one of your videos should be in a niche keyword targeted playlist. Like "Best Yoga Moves" or "Affiliate Marketing Applications". You should never have a playlist listed live on your channel if it doesn't have any of your content in it. Any playlists like this make sure they are unlisted. Now you can utilize the video ranking playlist method described later in this book that incorporates your videos at the top of the watch list with other videos ranking for your keyword term below. This scenario is the only time you should have other people's content accessible live on your channel.

NOW WE WILL CONQUER VIDEO SEO.

VIDEO SEO
Tags/Hashtags
Titles/Descriptions
Closed Captions
Translations

CLICK THROUGH INTERACTIONS
Watchtime/Likes
Comments/Hearts
Shares/Subscribes

SYNDICATION
Backlinks/Embeds

CHANNEL SEO & AUTHORITY
Tags/About
Playlists
Niche Videos

Youtube Video

4 Video Ranking Factors Best Video
Marketing Agency

Video SEO:

Never age restrict content unless your content contains adult language or nudity. This setting will severely limit your viewership and recommendations.

Titles:

You have 100 characters available for your title - you want to restate variations of the keyword you want to rank for or be more descriptive.

Your target url should be posted in the 1st line of the description to drive clickthrough rates & conversions.

Every video should have a description. Try to max it out with informative keyword rich text up to 5000 characters. if you ever want to promote a product or website put your destination link in the 1st line of your description with a call to action. Then put your title restated. Up to 15 #hashtags. A list of your social links to encourage interaction and viewership retention/subscription.

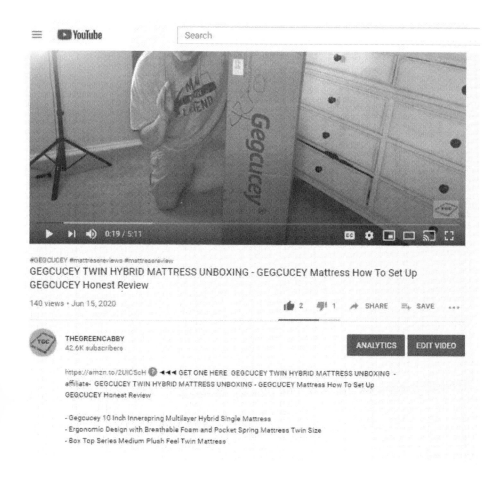

Youtube Video Description:

You have 5,000 characters that you can play around with here. This is your limit. The sweet spot for ranking seems to be between 2,000 and 4,000 characters. Yet, I often get pretty close to maxing out the limit, in order to promote my offer, three – five sentences describing the specific video content, have all the desired hashtags, my social links, niche related autogenerated ranking sentences or spun content from the leading websites for the niche topic and authority links at the bottom. At the end of the book I have provided the exact template that I have used to rank thousands of videos. This same temple is used for affiliate product review videos as well as ranking niche local business promotion videos.

Video Affiliate Disclaimers:

After creating videos for 12+ years, **collecting monthly checks from youtube for the millions of views** that we have gotten, let me tell you a little secret. You will always make more money as an affiliate, talking about a product that you love using, as apposed to adsense monetization from your youtube channel. Yes it is nice getting a monthly residual check from all the videos we have created. Yet, if you just decide to promote a few products on your channel that you are truly passionate about. The money that you can make, can far overshadow anything you could bring in from adsense.

If you are going to be promoting any type of products on your videos or in your descriptions, you will want to include 2 types of affiliate disclosures.

1) Near the link that you post; you will want to add an **-affiliate-** tag to make everyone aware that this link is promoted. Here is an example

Description ⑦

https://amzn.to/2UICScH ◄◄◄ GET ONE HERE GEGCUCEY TWIN HYBRID MATTRESS
UNBOXING -affiliate-   **Near the link, so that it is apparent this is a**
                                              promoted product

- Gegcucey 10 Inch I   pring Multilayer Hybrid Single Mattress
- Ergonomic Design wit   athable Foam and Pocket Spring Mattress Twin Size
- Box Top Series Medium Plush Feel Twin Mattress

2) You need to have a full affiliate disclaimer at the ***bottom of the video description***. This is to stay clear of any future regulations that youtube may clarify, as their current terms of service on the matter is quite vague. You also want to protect yourself from the new EU & California regulations that were recently passed. Cover your own @$$. Here is an example of one that I post in my video descriptions.

AFFILIATE DISCLOSURE (Example)

When you click on any of the links provided above, I may receive a small commission for recommending the item on the other end of the link. All products that I recommend, I do so on my own behalf without prompting from any manufacturer, company or retailer. If I recommend a product it is because I believe in what that product can do or be. All videos and content where recommendations are posted are for educational purposes only. You must do your due diligence and research when investing in a product for yourself or spending any type of capital.

#Hashtags:

Maximum number of #hashtags per video is 15. If you have more than 15 youtube will disregard all tags and will completely erase their ranking ability. Always put your 3 most important hashtags at the beginning of the list, as they will be put highlighted right below your video and will be given the most importance in ranking factors. ***You can see an example of the top 3 hashtags hyperlinked below a video in the picture above.*** Each #hashtag creates a separate search page that gives you the ability to rank a video in many more ways.

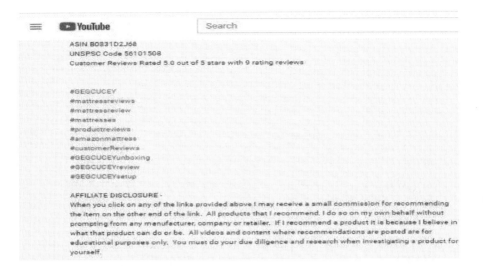

ASIN B0831D2J68
UNSPSC Code 56101508
Customer Reviews Rated 5.0 out of 5 stars with 9 rating reviews

#GEGCUCEY
#mattressreviews
#mattressreview
#mattresses
#productreviews
#amazonmattress
#customerReviews
#GEGCUCEYunboxing
#GEGCUCEYreview
#GEGCUCEYsetup

I put some great examples of how to set this up at the back of the book. I pulled these from TUBERANK JEET 4 PRO which is a paid software with the first upgrade (gives you 50 videos worth of hashtag search results). http://www.tuberanked.com This is the only app that pulls ***hashtags being used in videos*** for your keyword.

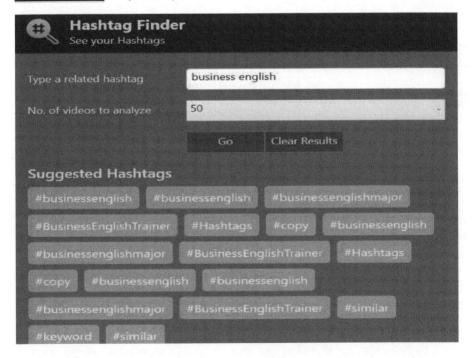

Hashtag Finder
See your Hashtags

Hashtags used in videos

#mmmEnglish #BusinessEnglish #PhrasalVerbs

#EnglishIdioms #EnglishLesson #RealEnglish

#EnglishTeacher #YouTubeTeacher #mmmEnglish

#BusinessEnglish #EnglishVocabulary #EnglishIdioms

#YouTubeTeacher #Lingoda #EnglishWithEmma

#EnglishCourse #BusinessEnglish #LearnEnglishGrammar

#EnglishClass101 #businessenglish #englishforwork

#englishwithniharika #businessenglish #businessenglishpod

#businessenglishcourse #Write #Emails #English

#EnglishClass101l #Vocabulary #LearnEnglish

TUBERANK

 Optimize Video
Follow the recommendations

 Hashtag Finder
See your Hashtags

 Home

 Optimize

 Discover

Analyze

Tag Finder

Hashtag Finder

Favorite Tags

Favorite Hashtags

Favorite Videos

Favorite Channels

Uploads

Metadata

Main Keyword

URL

Title   0/100

Description   0

Tags (Comma Seperated)   0/500

Type a related hashtag	communication skills
No. of videos to analyze	50

Go   Clear Results

Suggested Hashtags

#communicationskills #CommunicationSkills

#communicationskillscoach #communicationskillstraining

 #Hashtags #copy #communicationskills

#CommunicationSkills #communicationskillscoach

 #communicationskillstraining #Hashtags #copy

 #communicationskills #communicationskills

You can get a basic hashtag suggestion service (free) here https://tagsyoutube.com/hashtagsyoutube yet they **don't provide actual hashtags on youtube** but suggest hashtags that they think might be useful. You can also search for a #hashtag in the **youtube search bar** and see if any other video is using it by looking in the videos description.

Advanced Traffic Secret 2:

Translated closed captions and translated video descriptions will increase views and watch time 15%-45% percent, increase views and revenue (pictures included) the program I use is **Lingo blaster and Captionizer** - http://www.lingoblastr.com You can translate each video into the top 10 languages for your channel, out of 98 languages.

Subtitles and CC	Views ↓		Average view duration	Average percentage viewed	Watch time (hours)	
☐ Total	263,341		2:28	40.0%	10,877.0	
No subtitles/CC	241,964	91.9%	2:27	40.1%	9,905.3	91.1%
☐ English	11,113	4.2%	1:44	36.8%	322.1	3.0%
☐ Chinese (China)	3,279	1.3%	5:48	41.6%	317.7	2.9%
☐ Afrikaans	1,534	0.6%	2:13	54.9%	57.1	0.5%
☐ Spanish	1,154	0.4%	3:38	39.9%	70.2	0.7%
☐ Arabic	854	0.3%	1:50	33.4%	26.2	0.2%
☐ French	779	0.3%	3:41	38.1%	47.9	0.4%
☐ Hindi	700	0.3%	2:39	30.2%	30.9	0.3%
☐ German	533	0.2%	2:27	29.1%	21.9	0.2%
☐ Bangla	374	0.1%	3:02	63.3%	18.9	0.2%
☐ Filipino	368	0.1%	2:26	41.4%	15.0	0.1%
☐ Portuguese	358	0.1%	3:06	34.1%	18.5	0.2%
☐ Chinese (Taiwan)	110	0.0%	6:45	42.5%	12.4	0.1%
☐ Italian	90	0.0%	4:43	37.4%	7.1	0.1%

Summary

Last 28 days

Views	42.9K ↑	4%
Watch time (hours)	2.3K ↑	15%
Revenue	███████ ↑	10%

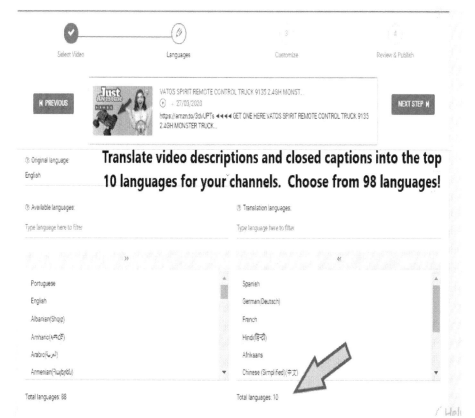

Select Video · Languages · Customize · Review & Publish

VATOS SPIRIT REMOTE CONTROL TRUCK 9135 2.4GH MONST...
· 27/03/2020
https://amzn.to/3dvUPTs ◀◀◀◀ GET ONE HERE VATOS SPIRIT REMOTE CONTROL TRUCK 9135 2.4GH MONSTER TRUCK...

◄ PREVIOUS   NEXT STEP ►

Translate video descriptions and closed captions into the top 10 languages for your channels. Choose from 98 languages!

Original language:
English

Available languages:
Type language here to filter

Portuguese
English
Albanian(Shqip)
Amharic(ኣማርኛ)
Arabic(العربية)
Armenian(Հայերէն)

Total languages: 88

Translation languages:
Type language here to filter

Spanish
German(Deutsch)
French
Hindi(हिन्दी)
Afrikaans
Chinese (Simplified)(中文)

Total languages: 10

/ Help

N PREVIOUS

VATOS SPIRIT REMOTE CONTROL TRUCK 9135 2.4GH MONST...

⊙ - 27/03/2020

https://amzn.to/3dvUPTs ◄◄◄◄ GET ONE HERE VATOS SPIRIT REMOTE CONTROL TRUCK 9135 2.4GH MONSTER TRUCK...

PUBLISH N

SPANISH   GERMAN(DEUTSCH)   FRENCH   HINDI(हिन्दी)   AFRIKAANS   CHINESE (SIMPLIFIED)(中文)

FILIPINO   NEPALI(नेपाली)   PUNJABI(ਪੰਜਾਬੀ)   URDU(اردو)

Translated Title:

Vatos spirit रिमोट कंट्रोल ट्रक 9135 2.4GH monster ट्रक क

Translated Description:

Https://amzn.to/3dvUPTs 9 एक यहीं प्राप्त करें vatos spirit रिमोट कंट्रोल ट्रक 9135 2.4GH monster ट्रक का उपयोग कैसे करें सबसे बेहतर समीक्षा-का उपयोग करें.

VATOS 1/12 RC आसान ट्रक ऑफ रोड रिमोट कंट्रोल करें Rechargeable 2.4GHz जायट रिमोट कंट्रोल कार 2WD मोटरग्रूप और टैंक रिमोट कंट्रोल कार | 36+ केंपीएच 26 एस्मीएच रिमोट कंट्रोल ट्रक | बच्चों और वयस्कों के लिए आदर्श करें

4WD RC ALL TERRAIN OFFROAD REMOTE CONTROL CAR-यद्यपि की सड़कें, घास का मैदान | जेतीं जमीन, बर्फ आदि शैलीलामें अन्नी भटकल बॉडी, रेल फेज और हाइड्रर कॉकपिट जैसे सभी इलाकों में खेलने के लिए तेज गति और अच्छा प्रदर्शन 1/12 आसान ट्रक | फोटर छन का डिजाइन कैमरा और लिए (वाहिक नहीं) रखने के लिए एक अच्छा मंच है।

4 व्हील सस्पेंशन और शॉकप्रूफ आसानी टेरिजन कार, 2.4 गीगाहर्ट्ज कंट्रोल सिस्टम-मजबूत मोटरग्रूप और कठिन, मजबूत रेस के लिए चार रेडियो खला निगरम जयाली 2.4 GHz रेडियो सिस्टम के साथ, आपको कभी भी अपर कार के साथ कोई रेडियो हस्तक्षेप नहीं मिलेगा | 60 मीटर की दूरी पर रिमोट कंट्रोल।

vatos spirit रिमोट कंट्रोल ट्रक 9135 जायट स्पीड क्रिएटिव ट्रक और ऊंचाई क्षमता बैटरी-शक्तिशाली मेटल और उपयोगितावादी दिखने वाले रबर टायर के साथ, अधिकतम गति ती-आयन 9.6V 800mAh के लिए (24 MPH तक है) 6A शुरे जायट स्पीडर सिस्टम और उच्च तापमान संरक्षण जयाली के साथ डेस्कटॉप क्षैंटे गाड़ी।

CAPTIONIZER MODULE FOR THE TRANSLATIONS OF THE CLOSED CAPTIONS TAKES 3 CLICKS PER VIDEO

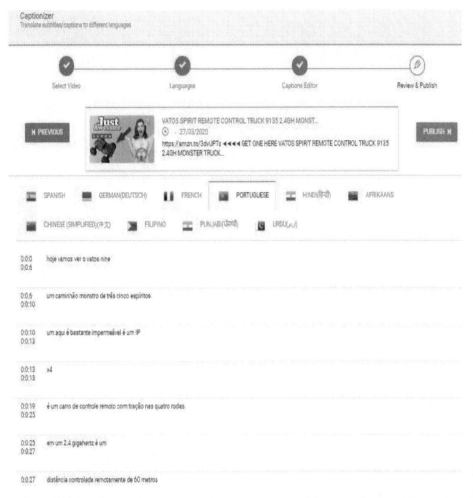

This will open up your video into different language ranking markets, giving you an advantage against those that don't make their videos available to other language speakers. If you only run one YT account it is $37 and the 3rd Upsell Is **VIDEO MARKETING BLASTER PRO** at $47 (I paid $120 for the regular and pro addon last year) - http://www.videomarketingblastr.com

This finds tags, competition, generates automatic ranking keyword description text, seo title suggestions for your keywords and tags. You can also use a video rank tracker. All described and pictured below. **These are my two main tools**, though I use MANY

Auto Generated Niche Keyword Ranking Sentences For Description

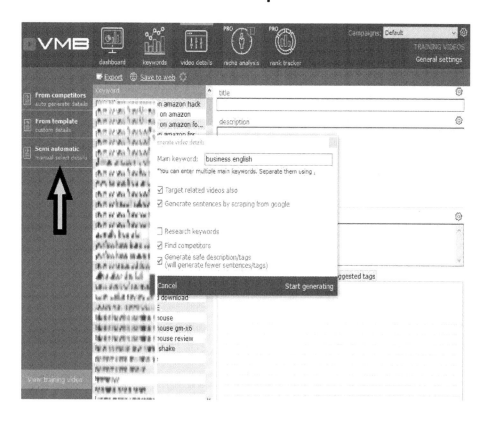

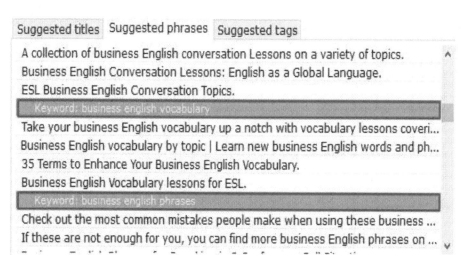

Tags:

Max out video tags 500 character, this is how people find your video & content. You need niche specific target longtail keywords that you want to try and rank for. Longtail keywords or keywords that have multiple related keywords are easier to rank for than a single keyword by itself.

Example:

Diet = Super Hard

How To Diet Properly = Super Easy

The more words in your keyword the easier it is to rank for.

Over time your channel and videos will gain authority from using the same or similar tags.

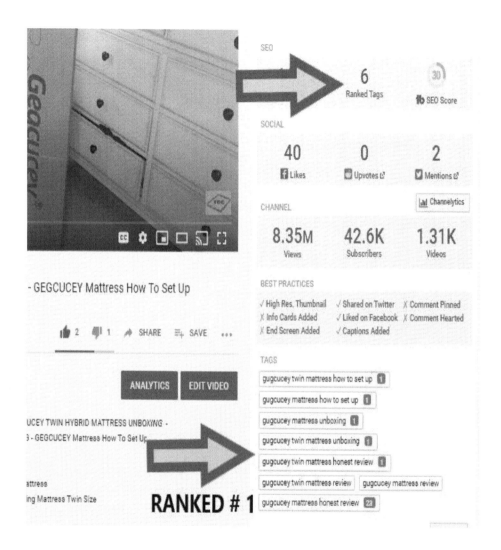

This is the main issue we see when videos are not getting ranked or receiving views. When you do your tags, you want to put anything you can think of that is related to your video that people might search for on google or youtube. This is how you are found. If google and youtube do not know what your video is about, they will not send you any viewers. I have attached pictures with examples on searching for keywords.

I pulled all the tags below, from VIDEO MARKETING BLASTER it is a paid software I use daily. http://www.videomarketingblastr.com links to google and youtube to give you youtube **keyword longtail tag rankings** and google search volume. This app also gives you keyword competition to see how hard it is to rank for specific keywords.

Keyword	Source	Rank	Search Results/YT Competing Vi...
business english	from longtail comp...	1,534	More than 1,000,000
business english conversation	from Tags, from Yo...	384	More than 1,000,000
business english vocabulary	from Tags, from Yo...	384	More than 1,000,000
business english phrases	from Tags, from Yo...	288	More than 1,000,000
business english speaking practice	from Tags	152	More than 1,000,000
how to speak business english flue...	from Tags	132	983,851
business english english	from longtail comp...	121	More than 1,000,000
negotiating in business english	from Tags	120	669,948
business english negotiation conve...	from Tags	120	More than 1,000,000
business english negotiation dialogue	from Tags	120	85,301
business english with 82 english	from longtail comp...	97	More than 1,000,000
business english meeting	from Tags	90	More than 1,000,000
business english dialogues	from Tags	90	More than 1,000,000
business english communication	from Tags	90	More than 1,000,000
learn business english	from Tags	90	More than 1,000,000
business english lesson	from Tags	90	More than 1,000,000
business english meetings	from Tags	90	More than 1,000,000
business english expressions	from Tags	90	More than 1,000,000
business english negotiations	from Tags	90	More than 1,000,000
negotiation business english	from Tags	90	921,959
in english business english	from longtail comp...	73	More than 1,000,000
basic english into business english	from longtail comp...	73	More than 1,000,000
business english podcast skills 360	from YouTube sugg...	68	8,446
business english podcasts macmillan	from YouTube sugg...	68	925
business english podcasts downloa...	from YouTube sugg...	68	More than 1,000,000
business english podcasts for begin...	from YouTube sugg...	68	More than 1,000,000
business english podcasts with tran...	from YouTube sugg...	68	4,220
business english podcasts free	from YouTube sugg...	68	530,793
basic business english course outline	from YouTube sugg...	68	More than 1,000,000
business english writing course outli...	from YouTube sugg...	68	330,275

You can use **TubeBuddy (FREE)** chrome/firefox extension **(YOU NEED THIS)** https://tinyurl.com/tubebuddyfree to get basic tag suggestions

You can also get some rough ideas from:

https://www.keyword.io/tool/youtube-longtail-finder

https://wassname.github.io/keywordshitter2/

https://neilpatel.com/ubersuggest/

CUSTOM THUMBNAILS:

Super important! TEXT on thumbnails: you want it to be short, BOLD & big. Your text should be interesting & DESCRIBE CONTENT. You will usually want a human face on your video thumbnail. The thumbnails stand out the most with facial expressions like, Surprised, Mad, Sad or Happy.

I am currently using a **Pro Thumbnail Maker** that is paid. http://www.thumbnailblast.com When you start making some YT money this is a good investment. Premade Pro Layered Thumbs that takes about **10 minutes to learn and 30 seconds to create**. So you can churn out pro quality thumbnails even with the **bold large letter stroke and shadows** that all the big youtubers use. Without having to learn or use Photoshop!

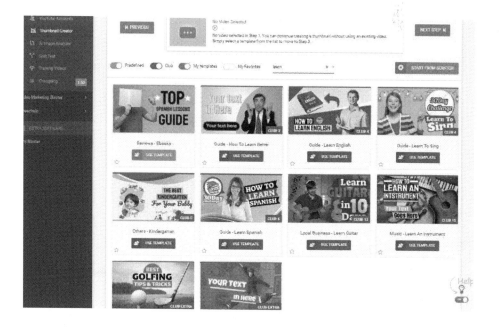

You can download the **TubeBuddy chrome extension https://tinyurl.com/tubebuddyfree** to use in the google chrome browser or firefox browser. I used this for years as it is free. This will allow you to create *simple custom thumbnails* with a background emojis and text

Advanced Traffic Secret :

Suggested and Related video and Playlist Strategy:

When you find the keyword that you want to target, you need to go into the top 3 videos and **COPY everything that is pertinent.** You want to tell youtube and google that these videos are so similar that they should be in the related videos right side bar. Once you get in the side bar, you want to make sure that your video is top notch content, so that it can stay there.

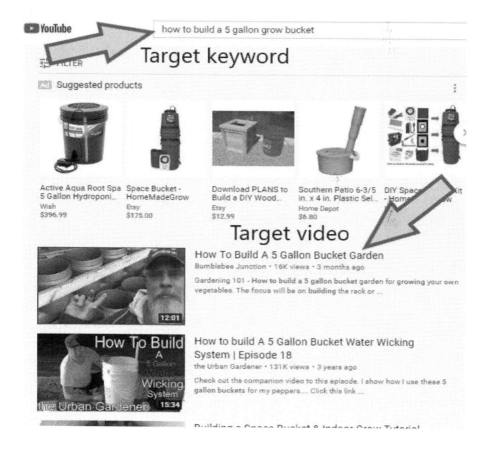

Then we are going to combine the video titles from the top 3 videos to create our video title.

Our Title would be: **How To Build A 5 Gallon Bucket Garden - Water Wicking System Building A Space Bucket Grow Tutorial**

Build the Related Video Description:

You are going to copy the tags exactly as they are in the number 1 video. Remember, we want them to think that these videos are so similar that they should be recommended together. To create our description, we are going to compile the descriptions exactly as they sit, just take out any kind of social links or personal info that they have. Now compile the #hashtags and then input the titles and channel names of the top 5 videos for the keyword search. Above these titles and name I would put the statement (Some of the other videos that inspired me to make this video:) to not look too spammy. Now youtube thinks, Wow look at this SIMILAR RELEVANT VIDEO!!!

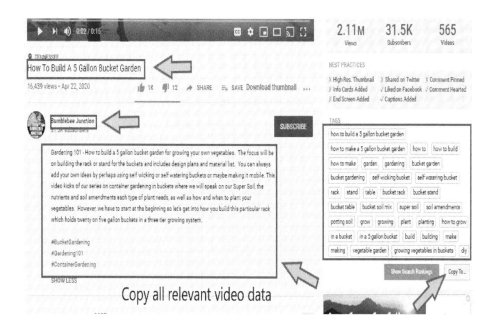

Copy all relevant video data

Our description would be:

How To Build A 5 Gallon Bucket Garden - Water Wicking System Building A Space Bucket Grow (title restated)

Gardening 101 - How to build a 5 gallon bucket garden for growing your own vegetables. The focus will be on building the rack or stand for the buckets and includes design plans and material list. You can always add your own ideas by perhaps using self wicking or self watering buckets or maybe making it mobile. This video kicks of our series on container gardening in buckets where we will speak on our Super Soil, the nutrients and soil amendments each type of plant needs, as well as how and when to plant your vegetables. However, we have to start at the beginning so let's get into how you build this particular rack which holds twenty on five gallon buckets in a three tier growing system.

In this episode we update on a few of our urban garden boxes, and we discuss and build a water wicking 5 gallon bucket. The ones we will be using on the rooftop to grow a large portion of our peppers. Let's Get Growing!

A complete breakdown of how to build a 5 gallon space bucket to grow medicinal CBD rich hemp as well as a time lapse video and step by step guide of my first indoor grow with this setup. Like the content?

Items I Used For This Grow:

VIPARSPECTRA 300W LED Grow Light.

MarsHydro 300W LED Grow Light.

Peat Pots.

Nature's Care Organic Gardening Soil / Potting Mix.

Perlite.

#BucketGardening

#Gardening101

#ContainerGardening

Some of the other videos that inspired me to make this video:

How To Build A 5 Gallon Bucket Garden by Bumblebee Junction

How to build A 5 Gallon Bucket Water Wicking System | Episode 18 by the Urban Gardener

Building a Space Bucket & Indoor Grow Tutorial by Hemp In A Pot

How to Build a Space Bucket, Part 1 Space Bucket Cannabis Grow by ILL GIL 710

How To Make A: Small Indoor Grow Bucket EASY by Let it sprout

Draw Attention to Your Suggested Video:

Draw attention to your Recommended Video by leaving the most recent comment, throw in a few emojis to draw the eye. Then like the comment to help become ranked as a relevant TOP comment. When people see your comment on the top and see that you also have a related video in the sidebar, it increases the likelihood of click thru to watch your video. The viewer clicking through to your video not only gets you the view and the watch time but it also tells youtube and google that your video is RELEVANT and related so they will continue to recommend your video and it might also go up in the organic rankings for exactly that reason.

Gardening 101 - How to build a 5 gallon bucket garden for growing your own vegetables. The focus will be on building the rack or stand for the buckets and includes design plans and material list. You can always add your own ideas by perhaps using self wicking or self watering buckets or maybe making it mobile. This video kicks of our series on container gardening in buckets where we will speak on our Super Soil, the nutrients and soil amendments each type of plant needs, as well as how and when to plant your vegetables. However, we have to start at the beginning so let's get into how you build this particular rack which holds twenty on five gallon buckets in a three tier growing system.

#BucketGardening
#Gardening101
#ContainerGardening

SHOW LESS

Draw attention to your Recommended Video by leaving the most recent comment, throw in a few emojis to draw the eye. Then like the comment to help become ranked as a relevant TOP comment

316
Comments

SORT
BY

 Add a public comment...

THEGREENCABBY 1 second ago

Loving how you built this, looks like a thousand bucket babies from the setup I did 7 years ago. Your build looks super heavy duty. Keep up the great work. I'm ringing that bell!

 1   REPLY

Get in that related section, rank over videos and channels with more views and higher authority.

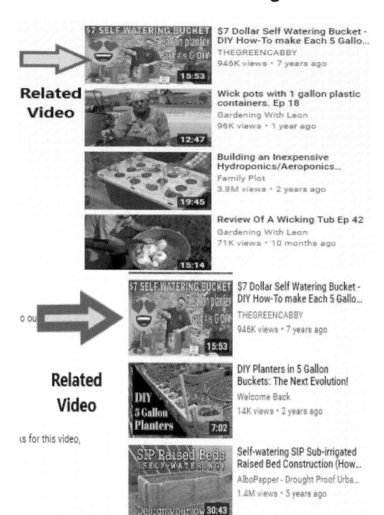

Getting in the related video sidebar is a huge part of my monthly watch time. Hop into your channel analytics and you can see what videos are recommending your video, what keywords people are searching for to find your video and the percentage of monthy views that are recommended by yotube. To get ther click your icon in the top right hand corner of the screen. Click "Youtube Studio". Click " Go To Channel Analytics" on the right side of your dashboard.

On my channel my videos get more Suggested video views than any other subset of view sources. **46.6% of my total channel views** and **57.4% of my total channel watch time** come right from the suggested video sidebar. That's right, **3.9 Million Views** scraped from the suggested sidebar and and **265 Thousand Watch Time hours**. Not too shabby. Would you suggest using this strategy?? Well let me show you how you can boost this strategy a little bit further.

Traffic source ▲	🔵	Impressions ▲	Impressions click-through rate ▲	Views ↓ ▲	Average view duration ▲	Watch time (hours) ▲
⬜ Total		24,826,521	5.5%	8,374,511	3:26	462,439.3
⬜ Suggested videos		7,893,924	5.9%	3,902,296 46.6%	4:14	265,642.4 57.4%
⬜ YouTube search		9,898,972	4.9%	1,424,150 17.0%	2:33	58,874.5 12.7%
⬜ Browse features		6,021,365	6.7%	1,131,814 13.5%	2:54	54,261.3 11.7%

Add the Playlist Strategy to the mix:

Any time you search for a keyword on youtube you get back a list that can consist of videos, related channels and playlists.

What is a playlist: "A playlist is a collection of video clips. Any person can make playlists and also share them. Do you intend to create a legendary weight room mix or your best-loved football touchdowns? What about distributing the very best food preparation video clips with your buddy?"

A playlist is essentially what it sounds like, a selection of video clips that continuously play in a predefined order. You can include your very own video clips or various other well-known video clips. What I truly like about playlists is that I am able to make 12 different playlists, aimed at 12 separate keyword phrases, while needing to publish just one video clip. Not just that, now we have an additional opportunity to rank with the playlist, yet we are "informing" YouTube that our video clip is "comparable" to the other video clips in our playlist. By doing this we obtain a much greater possibility to rank in the related or suggested video area of the various other video clips from our playlist.

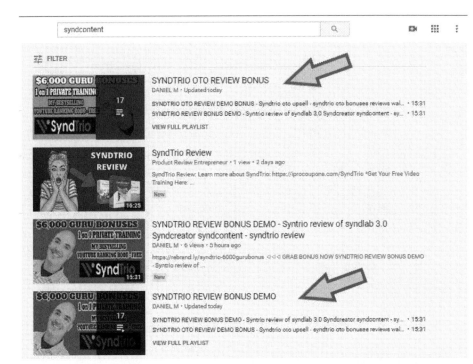

Similar to video clips, we need to ensure that we also have an excellent SEO optimized title and description for our playlist. Make certain to include your video clip as the first video in the playlist, afterwards include 2-3 additional video clips that you produced to target alternate keyword phrases. Then include the top ranking youtube videos, by view count, now you have essentially opened up the possibility of ranking your playlist as well as increasing the possibility of getting you video featured in the RELATED & SUGGESTED video column of some of the highest-ranking videos on your topic.

Curating "The Best Of"

You can additionally make use of playlist to curate 'the very best of' any type of given subject utilizing your very own video clips as well as other individual ones.

Consider details like.

- The Most Effective Pregnancy Workouts.
- The Most Effective Email Marketing Programs.
- Leading 12 Woodworkers in Las Vegas.

You can effortlessly broaden that, right into various other niches, that's just a few instances of ways you can rank with playlists.

YOUTUBE RANKING ALGORITHYM:

I **have ranked thousands of videos**; you can easily rank videos instantly. Depending on how videos perform the first 3 days will determine if google allows them to stay ranked.

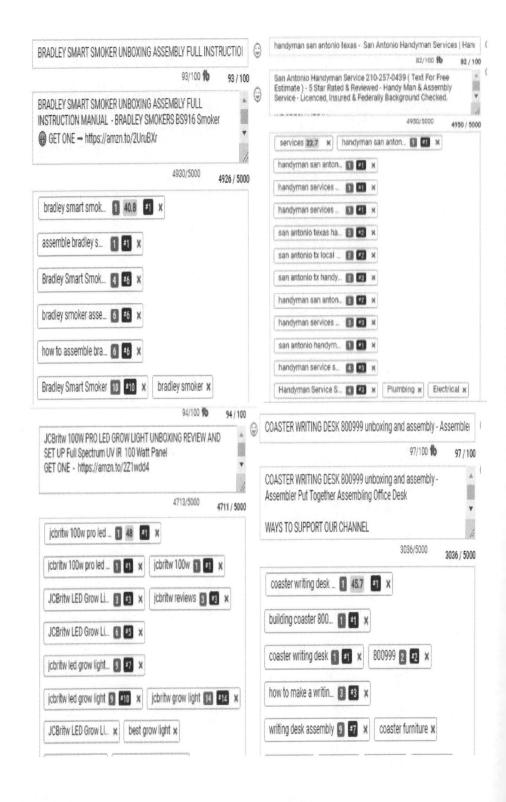

BRADLEY SMART SMOKER UNBOXING ASSEMBLY FULL INSTRUCTIOI

93/100

93 / 100

BRADLEY SMART SMOKER UNBOXING ASSEMBLY FULL INSTRUCTION MANUAL - BRADLEY SMOKERS BS916 Smoker
GET ONE → https://amzn.to/2UruBXr

4930/5000

4926 / 5000

bradley smart smok... 1 40.8 #1 x

assemble bradley s... 1 #1 x

Bradley Smart Smok... 0 #6 x

bradley smoker asse... 0 #6 x

how to assemble bra... 0 #6 x

Bradley Smart Smoker 10 #10 x   bradley smoker x

handyman san antonio texas - San Antonio Handyman Services | Hani

82/100   82 / 100

San Antonio Handyman Service 210-257-0439 (Text For Free Estimate) - 5 Star Rated & Reviewed - Handy Man & Assembly Service - Licenced, Insured & Federally Background Checked.

4950/5000   4950 / 5000

services 22.7 x   handyman san anton... 0 #1 x

handyman san anton... 1 #1 x

handyman services ... 0 #1 x

handyman services ... 0 #1 x

san antonio texas ha... 0 #2 x

san antonio tx local ... 2 #2 x

san antonio tx handy... 0 #2 x

handyman san anton... 0 #2 x

handyman services ... 0 #3 x

san antonio handym... 0 #1 x

handyman service s... 4 #3 x

Handyman Service S... 4 #3 x   Plumbing x   Electrical x

94/100   94 / 100

JCBritw 100W PRO LED GROW LIGHT UNBOXING REVIEW AND SET UP Full Spectrum UV IR 100 Watt Panel
GET ONE - https://amzn.to/2Z1wdd4

4713/5000   4711 / 5000

jcbritw 100w pro led ... 1 48 #1 x

jcbritw 100w pro led ... 1 #1 x   jcbritw 100w 1 #1 x

JCBritw LED Grow Li... 0 #3 x   jcbritw reviews 0 #3 x

JCBritw LED Grow Ll... 0 #5 x

jcbritw led grow light... 0 #7 x

jcbritw led grow light 0 #10 x   jcbritw grow light 14 #14 x

JCBritw LED Grow Ll... x   best grow light x

COASTER WRITING DESK 800999 unboxing and assembly - Assemblei

97/100   97 / 100

COASTER WRITING DESK 800999 unboxing and assembly - Assembler Put Together Assembling Office Desk

WAYS TO SUPPORT OUR CHANNEL

3036/5000   3036 / 5000

coaster writing desk ... 1 45.7 #1 x

building coaster 800... 0 #1 x

coaster writing desk 1 #1 x   800999 2 #2 x

how to make a writin... 0 #3 x

writing desk assembly 0 #7 x   coaster furniture x

Youtube's new ranking algorithm puts *click through rate and interactions* at the very top. Searching for your keyword in the youtube search bar, finding the video in the search results, clicking on it and watching the video all the way through (**Watchtime**). <u>**Always leave the first comment - like it – heart it - pin it – comment on it**</u>. This will increase video interactions and help youtube send you more traffic for your video.

The steps to follow when uploading a video for better ranking: **Commenting, Liking, Hearting Comments and then sharing on other social and blog platforms**.

NOW ITS TIME TO DOMINATE CLICK THROUGH VIDEO INTERACTIONS AND WATCHTIME

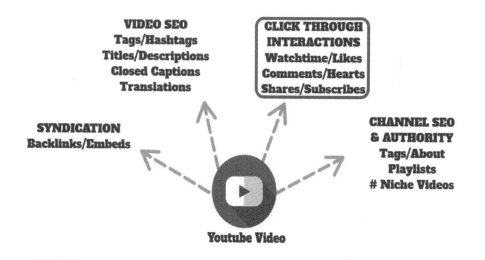

VIDEO SEO
Tags/Hashtags
Titles/Descriptions
Closed Captions
Translations

CLICK THROUGH
INTERACTIONS
Watchtime/Likes
Comments/Hearts
Shares/Subscribes

SYNDICATION
Backlinks/Embeds

CHANNEL SEO
& AUTHORITY
Tags/About
Playlists
Niche Videos

Youtube Video

4 Video Ranking Factors ▷ Best Video
Marketing Agency

EVERY VIDEO PUBLISHED: (greyhat ranking strategy)

Be the first like. Be the first comment: Include your link and call to action. LIKE the comment. HEART the comment. Comment on the comment.

With the Tubebuddy dashboard: share the video on **facebook**. Watch your video there. Share it on **twitter**. Watch your video there. Share it on **Medium**. Watch your video there. Share your video on **blogger**. Watch your video there. You will be well on your way to getting more traffic and watch-time. On your computer with your IP address you can also search for and watch your video on 3 different browsers while logged out of youtube. Once in the regular browser window and once in the incognito / private window of each browser.

EVERY VIDEO PUBLISHED: (blackhat ranking strategy)

For the **first three days**, right after posting your video start a PERSONA search and watch campaign. A ***persona*** is a google/youtube account that is each created on a different RESIDENTIAL IP ADDRESS and is then assigned a **dedicated/private proxy**. A dedicated/private proxy essentially tells google/youtube that this account has it's own computer. You access these account in a GHOSTBROWSER - http://www.ghostbrowsr.com which keeps each of these accounts logged in completely separate from each other *(essentially on their own computer each in a different city).*

Depending on the ranking difficulty: Search for your video in the youtube search bar with the KEYWORD you are trying to target, find the video and watch your video to completion with **15-35 different accounts EACH DAY for 3 Days (always different accounts each day).**

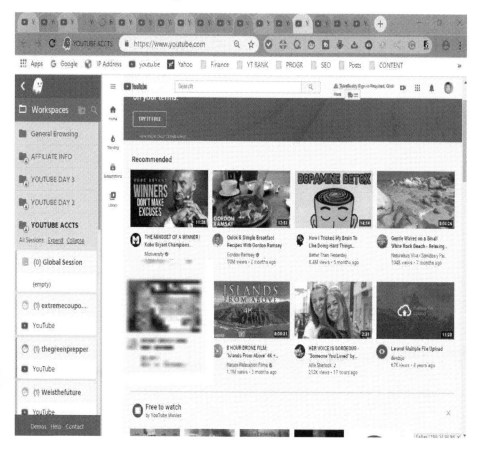

- **If you want to use the above strategy:** You will need a private/dedicated proxy for each youtube account.
- I currently use http://www.stormproxys.com . This dedicated proxy account should always stay the same and attached to only one youtube account. You can use the proxy for other tasks on other sites, yet with youtube it should always stay on that one account. Ghostbrowser will allow the accounts to stay logged in.

- Where with one click you can start watching videos, commenting and liking. If you want Likes to stick and makes sure the views and comments to stay. You will need 1 dedicated/private proxy per account.

NOW IT IS TIME TO CONQUER BACKLINKS AND EMBEDS

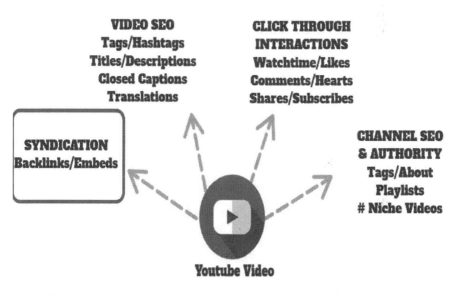

VIDEO SEO
Tags/Hashtags
Titles/Descriptions
Closed Captions
Translations

CLICK THROUGH INTERACTIONS
Watchtime/Likes
Comments/Hearts
Shares/Subscribes

SYNDICATION
Backlinks/Embeds

CHANNEL SEO & AUTHORITY
Tags/About
Playlists
Niche Videos

Youtube Video

4 Video Ranking Factors

Best Video
Marketing Agency

Backlinks and Automation:

Backlinks and video embeds are still a huge ranking factor for videos both on youtube and google.

1) Create social accounts, with the same name as your youtube account, that can automatically create backlinks and traffic to your videos and website.
   - **Twitter**
   - **Facebook**
   - **Pinterest**
   - **Medium (Blog)**
   - **Tumblr (Blog)**
   - **Blogger (Blog)**
   - **Wordpress (Blog)**

FIND OUT IF THE SAME NAME IS AVAILABLE ON ALL SOCIAL NETWORKS - http://knowem.com/ **(free)** type in your desired screenname here and it will show you if they are available on all social networks.

You want to add your social links in each video description to:

1) This adds social engagement and sharing

2) It also creates natural back links to these properties. (most people don't understand this) Let's just say it is a way for google and other search engines to give you a higher authority in search rankings which drives you more traffic. TRAFFIC MEANS MONEY, VIEWS and ENGAGEMENT!

When Posting Your Youtube Video on Social:

Twitter Template for Video Posting:

Remember you have 280 character. Use this room to help rank tweets and to be found in twitter search. The best way to be found in twitter search is by using hashtags. Here is the template I use. Also, your FIRST link will always show a preview. You notice I said first link. You can add a second link at the bottom to your website or main youtube channel landing page. This will help build authority and some passive social traffic when people decide to read your whole tweets.

Video Title – (Short youtube link)

#hashtag1

#hashtag2

#hashtag3

#hashtag4

#hashtag5

Link # 2

Facebook Template For Video Posting:

You will have no problem posting your lengthy content here as you can have 63,206 characters in your post. Literally a novel that no one will ever read. As with twitter you can also maximize #hashtags to get more traffic to your post. With Facebook you are limited to 3 hashtags that will rank. Don't use anymore as they will not help you. Each #hashtag actually creates its own search URL withing facebook that are populated with other posts of the same hashtag. Very powerful way to get through the hordes of posts on facebook. Find something trending and relevant!

Video Title – (Short youtube link)

1-2 sentences describing the content.

#hashtag1

#hashtag2

#hashtag3

Instagram

You are only able to have one hyper link on your profile and no links on your videos, unless you have a large following. We suggest that you put your short website link inside your video or drive people to your profile page that can link out to a page with multiple links or your money site/landing page.

FREE AUTOMATION:

After you set up your social profiles, with all the names matching you can go to IFTT.com create a free account. & set up automatic actions that happen once you upload a video to youtube & make it public. (THIS WILL GET YOU MUCH MORE ENGAGEMENT - BACKLINKS FOR RANKING - SAVE YOU TIME)

The automatic actions you want to set up are

Once youtube video is published   Post TITLE & LINK TO TWITTER

Once youtube video is published   Post TITLE & LINK 3 #HASHTAGS to
FACEBOOK PAGE

Once youtube video is published   Post TITLE LINK to TUMBLR BLOG

Once youtube video is published   Post TITLE LINK 3 #HASHTAGS to PINTEREST
POST

Post your New Instagram videos   to Twitter

Post your Instagram photos as native Twitter photos when #twitter is in the
caption

NEW TWITTER FOLLOWER   Thank new twitter follower

WISH FOLLOWERS HAPPY NEW YEAR

*THESE ALL CREATE SYNDICATION BACKLINKS TO YOUR YOUTUBE VIDEOS
(IMPORTANT TO GOOGLE)*

Instant Backlinks Engagement and Traffic:

With the **TubeBuddy chrome or Firefox extension** you can *share on 5 social profiles*, see how many characters you have left when creating your tags, titles and descriptions. https://tinyurl.com/tubebuddyfree You can also see the tags other people use when you watch their video. (What we showed you in the Suggested Video Strategy.) This would be helpful to you so that you can see tags from competing videos and copy, and can learn what successful viral videos are using as tags.

Mass Backlinks & Video Embeds: (greyhat strategy)

To this day one of the most effective ways to boost your video rankings on google and edge up your rankings in youtube is by having **backlinks and video embeds on social networks, blogs and bookmarking sites**. This strategy does take a little work but can go a long way to building you channel authority. There are 30 sites where you can post the link to your vide, the video embed and written content about your video. You take 5 minutes to enter in all of the required info and can automatically syndicate your video and video links to all of the sites with one button click.

If you create multiple accounts on the 25 sites you can exponentially increase the number of backlinks and video embeds for each youtube video posted. This strategy will help build channel and video authority over time as well as helping rankings of the videos posted on youtube. Especially for harder to rank terms. SYNDLAB + SYNBUDDY + SYNDCREATOR + SYNDCONTENT For a one time price (I was able to secure a **backdoor discount using the promo code SYNDLAB**) you can get **2,000 syndications each and every month, forever**. The front end account come with 100 accounts automatically created for you and 2000 pieces of auto-generated content when you post syndications. http://www.syndtreo.com

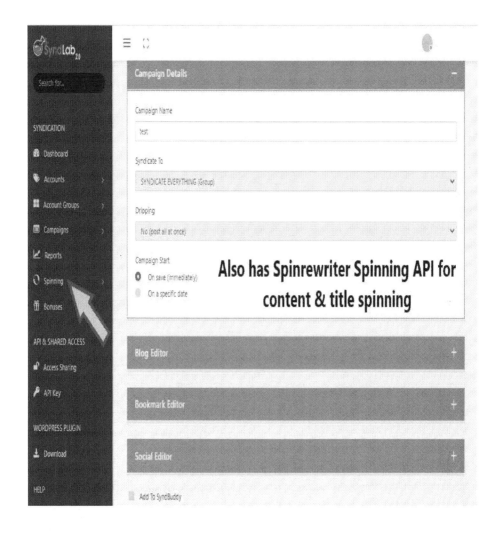

You can have the accounts auto created to use in the syndlab system, they just had a new addition to this program released called **Syndtrio**. http://www.syndtreo.com It comes with the above syndlab + Synbuddy. It also comes with SyndCreator - Automatic Account Creation (with NO proxies or captcha costs needed) & SyndContent - Automatic Content Generation. This part of the system is a credit-based system.

SyndCreator	SyndContent	SyndLab
Automatic Account Creation	Automatic Content Generation	Automatic Content Syndication

SyndCreator auto generates accounts on 25 different networks, allowing you to syndicaton on platforms that do, blogging, bookmarking, video hosting, pdf hosting, picture hosting. A wide variety of backlinks can now be pointed at your website or video with a few minutes of setup.

SyndCreator

- Dashboard
- Account Creation
- Sub Accounts
- Admin

| Details | Sites | Profile | Mail | Syndlab |

Sites
Which Sites Should We Create Accounts On?

Your Credits: 100 Selected Cost: 0

Type: Blog
- ApSense
- Evernote
- Joomla
- LiveJournal
- Skyrock
- Tumblr
- Wordpress

Type: Bookmark
- Bibly
- Instapaper
- Papaly
- Pearltrees
- Private - EnerCell
- Private - HealthyDome
- Private - WorldOfFootball
- SiteJot

Type: Pdf
- Annotale
- FreePDFHosting

Type: Photo
- Photobucket
- WeHeartIt

Type: Social
- DeviantArt
- Ello
- MySpace
- Twitter

Type: Video
- Dailymotion

25 Different Platforms that auto create accounts for mass syndictation

SyndContent auto creates autogenerated sentence or paragraph content, that can be spun and used on hundreds of accounts on 25 platforms.

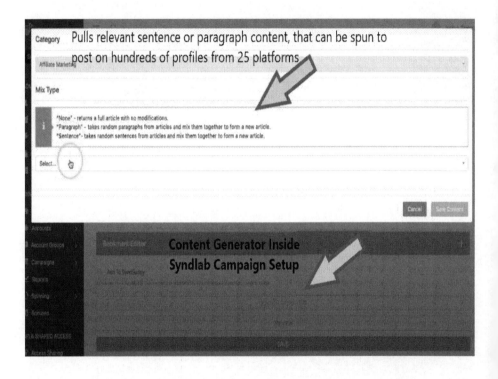

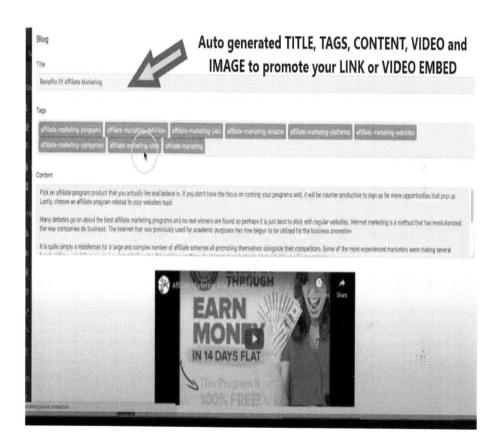

Syndtrio. http://www.syndtreo.com

Youtube Mass Video Marketing: (blackhat strategy)

This is where the whole game changes. Mass video marketing is not something to use with your main youtube channel. Before you read any further, let me say again. DON'T DO THIS WITH YOUR MAIN ACCOUNT!

Youtube Mass Video Marketing gives you the opportunity to create thousands of videos, traffic driving backlinks and local business citations, monthly on autopilot. You can point these automatically created videos and the traffic they create at any phone number, website, authority youtube channel or youtube video. To be exact, with the base account, you can have up to 3,000 videos created and uploaded each and every month.

http://www.massvideouploads.com Full training provided there.

Direct access to the app at http://yiveapp.com

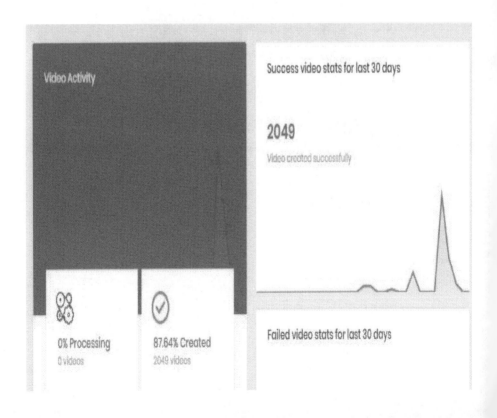

Type ⬦	Distribution ⬦	Per Day ⬦	Active ⬦	Uploaded	Updated At ⬦
Spintax	Auto Upload	2	On	35/86	20 hours ago
Spintax	Auto Upload	2	On	39/93	20 hours ago
Spintax	Auto Upload	2	On	35/102	20 hours ago
Spintax	Auto Upload	1	On	23/102	20 hours ago
Spintax	Auto Upload	1	On	35/96	20 hours ago
Spintax	Auto Upload	1	On	33/96	20 hours ago
Spintax	Auto Upload	1	On	43/97	20 hours ago
Spintax	Auto Upload	20	On	311/2780	15 hours ago
Spintax	Auto Upload	20	On	309/2780	15 hours ago
Spintax	Auto Upload	2	On	75/88	20 hours ago
Spintax	Auto Upload	2	On	87/125	20 hours ago

50 ⬦ Showing

	Uploading	46%	RELAXIN spintax	2 seconds ago
❯	Uploaded		Archety spintax	3 seconds ago
	Uploaded		Vibrati spintax	13 seconds ago
	Processing Upload	99%	Manefes spintax	19 seconds ago
	Uploaded		Manefes spintax	54 seconds ago
	Uploaded		YogaBur spintax	1 minute ago
	Uploaded		Panic A spintax	2 minutes ago
	Uploaded		Archety spintax	3 minutes ago
	Uploaded		MAN CLI spintax	15 hours ago
	Uploaded		MAN CLI spintax	15 hours ago

You get youtube accounts that are double pva verified (verified by phone), each account should be created on a separate residential proxy ip. Each account has a unique profile picture created by This Person Does Not Exist. https://thispersondoesnotexist.com This website gives you AI generated photos that are unique and have never been seen before on google or anywhere else. Each account should also be subscribed to mailing lists, to look like normal accounts.

Once you get your accounts, put them in the auto video generating app and let them season for 14 days. Seasoning means the app will do human like actions, such as checking emails, watching videos, subscribing to yt channels and various other tasks. (Don't log into these accounts on your computer as you can get your computer ip address banned by the "BIG G" or getting all of these accounts closed)

Status	Channels	Videos	Seasoning Duration ↓	Actions
Connected	1	0	• 12 days	🗎 🖉 🗑
Connected	1	0	• 12 days	🗎 🖉 🗑
Connected	1	0	• 12 days	🗎 🖉 🗑
Connected	1	0	• 12 days	🗎 🖉 🗑
Connected	1	0	• 12 days	🗎 🖉 🗑

Once your accounts are seasoned and ready to start uploading, you can choose one of the many types of campaigns that auto generate videos for posting. The 8 types of video campaigns you have to choose from are.

- **Amazon Video Campaign**
- **RSS Feed Video Campaign**
- **Keyword Video Campaign**
- **Auto Dealer Video Campaign**
- **Spintax Video Campaign**
- **Specific URL Video Campaign**
- **Multiple URLs Video Campaign**
- **Use Your Own Video Remix Campaign**

Name of your Campaign

Enter campaign name

Choose Campaign Type

○ Amazon	AMAZON	○ RSS Feed	CASTER
Automatically create video reviews of Amazon products		Create videos automatically RSS Feeds	

○ Keyword	CASTER	○ Auto Dealer	CASTER
Create videos automatically from keywords		Create vehicle videos from autotrader.com	

○ Specific URL	SMB	○ Spintax Videos	SMB
Promote any products or services from any specific URL		Promote any products or services using Spintax content	

○ Use Your Own Video Remix	SMB	○ Multiple Urls	SMB
Promote your own multiple assets using multiple Keywords		Promote your own video using multiple urls	

Our absolute favorite campaigns for generating affiliate sales, Local business marketing rankings and driving traffic to CPA offers

 NEXT STEP

Take over whole search terms, like here where we had the first 99 search results and pushed the rest of the competition several pages down.

Search results blurred to protect client and niche.

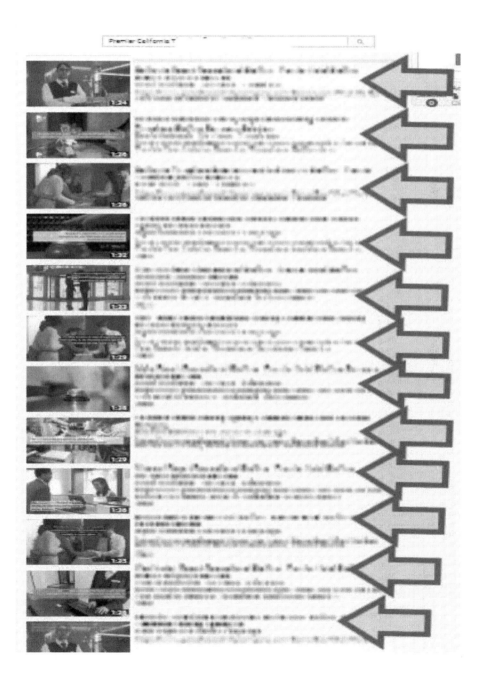

Or you can decide to scoop up affiliate earnings as you have a video auto created for every target keyword for the products you are targeting.

JVZoo.com	Inbox	[Cha-Ching] You've been paid $13.50
JVZoo.com	Inbox	[Cha-Ching] You've been paid $18.50
JVZoo.com	Inbox	[Cha-Ching] You've been paid $23.50
JVZoo.com	Inbox	[Cha-Ching] You've been paid $18.50

Financials

Next estimated payment

$400.20

Commission in Approval

$0.00

Previous payments received

$8,183.04

Commission Reward

Get 15% when customers purchase using your referral link within 30 **day(s)**.

ⓘ Sales are estimated in USD. Actual sales and commissions may be in a different currency.

Financials

Next estimated payment

$38.72

Commission in Approval

$0.00

Previous payments received

$802.72

Commission Reward

Get **10%** when customers purchase using your referral link within **14 day(s)**.

ⓘ Sales are estimated in USD. Actual sales and commissions may be in a different currency.

Reports

Fee Schedule | Payment History | Download Reports | Feedback | Help

Apr 15 2020 - Jul 13 2020 / Custom Date Range ⌄   Tracking ID: Multiple ⌄

Last Updated: Jul 12 2020 +00:00

Summary	Fees	Bounties
$91.75	$91.75	$0.00

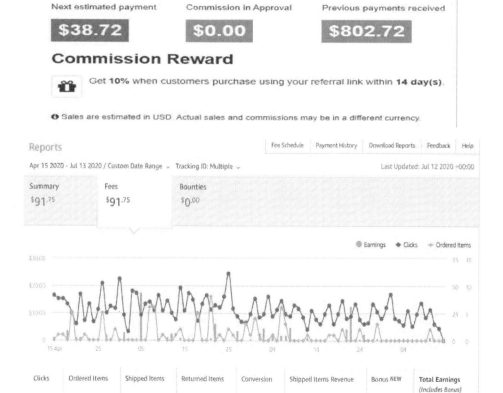

● Earnings   ◆ Clicks   ＋ Ordered Items

Clicks	Ordered Items	Shipped Items	Returned Items	Conversion	Shipped Items Revenue	Bonus NEW	Total Earnings (Includes Bonus)
2,492	79	74	1	3.17%	$2,743.27	$0.00	$91.75

Dominate local search terms, and take over whole niches with just 10-15 minutes work per campaign.

If we have time I'd like to show me about how I can show my client what the campaign is doing for his business. Since You started the YIVE campaign his business got a lot of traffic and he went from 2 days only to be open at the new location to 4 days now from Monday to Thursday so it's time for me to show him this new campaign , instead of FB ADS, it's getting him clients...

938 videos uploaded of 5560 videos total on 30 accounts

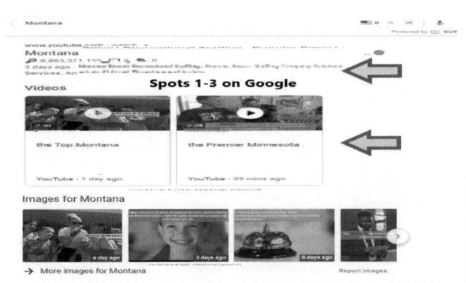

Montana

Spots 1-3 on Google

Videos

the Top Montana

the Premier Minnesota

YouTube - 1 day ago

YouTube - 39 mins ago

Images for Montana

→ More images for Montana

Report images

Trained google to create a carousel linking to our content

http://www.massvideouploads.com Full training provided there.

LIVE EVENT RANKING

This is strategy works great for local marketing, where you can put a PHONE NUMBER on your thumbnail to drive calls. This is very effective, because when you post a live event, youtube and google usually put a higher importance on these, even if they are just scheduled.

So, you can jump the line, ahead of all the other ranking videos to rank your posted live event on the first page of google and youtube. BE CAREFUL, you don't want to post more than 3 live events per day to keep your account safe and in good standing.

Also, the strategy here is to NEVER ACTUALLY STREAM the videos. Let them rank with a ***Call To Action***, to drive traffic to your link, landing page or phone number. This is also very effective if you have something everyone wants like a discount, coupon or exclusive deal. You can build your email list with a landing page. And then give them what they seek.

---

funnel lingo blaster	🎤 🔍

Videos

funnel lingo blaster - lingo blaster 2.0 review demo $2975 ...	demo lingo blaster - lingo blaster review - lingo blaster review ...	lingo blaster discount - lingo blaster review lingo blaster ...
DANIEL M	DANIEL M	DANIEL M
YouTube - 3 days ago	YouTube - 2 days ago	YouTube - 2 days ago

lingoblaster.com › ... ▾
JV | Lingo Blaster
Get JVZoo Aff Link; Email Swipes. Join Us On February 16th For the EPIC Launch Of **Lingo Blaster** 2.0. New Contest + Improved **Funnel** + High Scarcity ...

www.thenewsfunnel.com › lingo-blaster-2-review ▾
Lingo Blaster 2 Review | The News Funnel
4 days ago - **Lingo Blaster** 2 ReviewSee Full **Lingo Blaster** 2 Review At: https://internetcloning.com/**lingo-blaster**-2-review/

Images for funnel lingo blaster

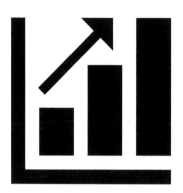

Basic FREE Rank Tracking:

Once you have all the fundamentals of the tags, title and descriptions, you can post your video and check the ranking to see if you rank for any of your keywords and tags that you are targeting.

https://tubetool.io/

https://ytrank.net

Regular Video Ranking Template

DESCRPTION:
{URL or Phone Number} - [CALL TO ACTION] {title Copy & Pasted}

3 sentences describing video content.

COMPANY NAP (Name Address Phone)

Social Links:
Linkedin
Facebook
Twitter
Instagram
Snapchat
Blogger/Wordpress

Top 3 #HASHTAGS
12 More related hashtags.

3 Paragraphs KEYWORD RICH Niche Specific sentences.
(can be same for each video/ Can SPIN for better results – no one reads this far except youtube and google)
General Channel Topic Content Paragraph {Video keyword at end of each paragraph with a period}.
General Channel Topic Content Paragraph {Video keyword at end of each paragraph with a period}.
General Channel Topic Content Paragraph {Video keyword at end of each paragraph with a period}.

Thank you for watching { Video title Copy & Pasted}. {Short Video Link}

Authority link:
(#1 ranked video, #1 ranked website on google for video keyword term, Wikipedia Topic URL)

TAGS: {video keyword}, 400 character longtail niche specific tags

YOUR VIDEO TEMPLATE EXAMPLE

http://www.website.com – **Click For Business English Communication Skills & Personal Branding**
{title}

{3 Sentences describing the video in your own words}

Social Links:
Linkedin:
Facebook:
Twitter:
Instagram:
Snapchat:
Blogger/Wordpress

#BusinessEnglish
#BusinessEnglishTrainer
#BusinessEnglishLesson
#BusinessEnglishCourse
#EnglishforBusiness
#EnglishForWork
#PhrasalVerbs
#EnglishIdioms
#EnglishLesson
#EnglishVocabulary
#LearnEnglishGrammar
#EnglishConversation
#BasicEnglishSpeaking
#CommunicationSkills
#CommunicateWithConfidence

Hi, I'm Betty Johnson. Your Personal Business English Coach.

My Story

Having worked in the Square Mile in **London** at the hub of the financial sector in marketing management, I have experienced first-hand, how communication has an incredible impact on your professionalism and your effectiveness in international business.

With almost 20 years of management training experience and a passion for using communication to make a great impression, I give you the skills, practice, feedback and confidence to perform in any business conversation. It's time for you to show up as the expert – internationally!

Business English is not rocket science. Thanks to my unique blended learning approach you will soon be speaking and thinking in English. **Let's meet online for a cup of tea.**

Business English Authority Building Ranking Text

A collection of business English conversation Lessons on a variety of topics. Business English Conversation Lessons: English as a Global Language. ESL Business English Conversation Topics that you can enjoy learning from.

Take your business English vocabulary up a notch with vocabulary lessons covering everything from finance to HR. Business English vocabulary topics that will help you learn new business English words and phrases. Business English Vocabulary lessons for ESL.

Whatever your workplace, our business English course will equip you with the valuable skills needed to communicate effectively. The Business English course is designed to prepare students to use English in a present or future work situation.

Business English lessons are targeted for people with office jobs. ESL Business English Lessons about advertising and marketing. We hope you enjoy the free business English conversation lesson.

EXAMPLE VIDEO TAGS:

Business English, Business English Trainer, Business English Lesson, Business English Course, English for Business, English For Work, Phrasal Verbs, English Idioms, English Lesson, English Vocabulary, Learn English Grammar, English Conversation, Basic English Speaking, business english conversation, business english vocabulary, business english phrases, business english speaking practice, business english dialogues, business english communication, business english lesson, basic english into business english, business english phrases and idioms, english for business, how to negotiate in English

MASS VIDEO APP Video Ranking Template (AFFILIATE or LOCAL)

TITLE:
{keyword} - {buy|Get|purchase} this {now|right now|Right away}

DESCRPTION:
{SPUN URL 1 per 25}/Phone Number - [CALL TO ACTION] {title}
3 sentences
{1,2,3|2,1,3|3,2,1}

COMPANY NAP
(Name Address Phone)

Top 3 #HASHTAGS
Spin the rest of the hashtags.
{##|##}
SPUN DESCRIPTION {keyword}.
SPUN DESCRIPTION {keyword}.
SPUN DESCRIPTION {keyword}.
SPUN DESCRIPTION {keyword}.
Thank you for watching {keyword}.
Authority link

TAGS:
{keyword},400 character longtail niche specific tags

It is now time to take your new knowledge and start dominating youtube video niches one at a time!!

DAILY USE PROGRAMS:

- Auto generated Keyword Sentences for descriptions, Long-tail Keyword Research: http://www.videomarketingblastr.com **(Pro Lifetime)**
- Only App That pulls Youtube #HASHTAGS being used on videos **(Pro Does up to 50 video search)**: http://www.tuberanked.com
- Count Characters Description up to 5,000 characters, Title up to 100 and Tags up to 500 characters : https://wordcounter.net/character-count
- Professional thumbnail creator with 3 click Templates: http://www.thumbnailblast.com
- Best Text To Speech Realistic Voices better the Google Voice and Amazon Polly (Pro does up to 20,000 Characters) : http://www.speechilo.com **(Pro Upsell Page Select NO NOT INTERESTED at the bottom of the page to get a LIFETIME onetime offer)**
- Translate Closed Captions & Description into your choice of up to 10 languages of 102 : http://www.lingoblastr.com **(Increases Watch Time and Retention between 15%-45%)**
- Stock footage video creation software : http://www.vidnamii.com **(14 Day Free Trial)**
- Make all first letters or even entire words CAPITALIZED: https://convertcase.net/
- Append a prefix or suffix to lines A WORD BEFORE OR AFTER ALL TEXT: https://rebrand.ly/appendprefix
- Keyword lists New line to comma, or Comma to new line: https://sortmylist.com/
- Best Content & Text Spinning: http://www.spinrewritr.com **(60% Discount 5 Day Free Trial)**
- Most affordable Quality Dedicated/Private Proxies http://www.stormproxys.com

Join Us On Facebook To Mastermind On Youtube Growth & Making Passive Income

https://www.facebook.com/groups/passivecashstacker

FREE MASSIVE YOUTUBE THANK YOU BONUS

https://rebrand.ly/yourbookbonus

Thank you for your purchase and your support!

30 DAY CHANNEL BUILDER CHALLENGE

Create 1 video per day, for 30 days, to kick start your growth and channel authority. Build your videos all in the same niche to maximize growing authority. You can use the video storyboard templates to work out your ideas. Each video should have 3 parts, no matter your niche. The INTRO/HOOK, STORY & CALL TO ACTION. The call to action will be subscribe, download my free ebook or course, click the link in the description. Give your viewers something to do after the video. Drive engagement and interactions, as this is a huge part of the new youtube video ranking algorithm.

_____

_____

_____

_____

_____

Intro

_____

_____

_____

_____

Story

_____

_____

_____

_____

Call To Action

Intro

Story

Call To Action

	Intro
_____	
_____	
_____	
_____	
_____	
_____	**Story**
_____	
_____	
_____	
_____	**Call To Action**
_____	
_____	
_____	
_____	

Intro

Story

Call To Action

_____

_____

_____

_____

_____

Intro

_____

_____

_____

_____

_____

Story

_____

_____

_____

_____

_____

Call To Action

_____

Intro

Story

Call To Action

_____

_____

_____

_____

_____

_____

Intro

_____

_____

_____

_____

_____

Story

_____

_____

_____

_____

_____

Call To Action

_____

Intro

Story

Call To Action

_____

_____

_____

_____

_____

_____

Intro

_____

_____

_____

_____

_____

Story

_____

_____

_____

_____

Call To Action

_____

Intro

Story

Call To Action

_____

_____

_____

_____

_____

Intro

_____

_____

_____

_____

Story

_____

_____

_____

_____

Call To Action

_____

Intro

Story

Call To Action

_____

_____

_____

_____

_____

Intro

_____

_____

_____

_____

_____

Story

_____

_____

_____

_____

_____

Call To Action

_____

Intro

Story

Call To Action

_____

_____

_____

_____

_____

_____

Intro

_____

_____

_____

_____

Story

_____

_____

_____

_____

Call To Action

_____

Intro

Story

Call To Action

Intro

Story

Call To Action

Intro

Story

Call To Action

_____

_____

_____

_____

Intro

_____

_____

_____

_____

Story

_____

_____

_____

_____

Call To Action

_____

Intro

Story

Call To Action

Intro

Story

Call To Action

Intro

Story

Call To Action

_____

_____

_____

_____

_____

Intro

_____

_____

_____

_____

_____

Story

_____

_____

_____

_____

Call To Action

_____

Intro

Story

Call To Action

_____

_____

_____

_____

_____

Intro

_____

_____

_____

_____

_____

Story

_____

_____

_____

_____

_____

Call To Action

_____

Intro

Story

Call To Action

Intro

Story

Call To Action

Intro

Story

Call To Action

_____

_____

_____

_____

_____

Intro

_____

_____

_____

_____

_____

Story

_____

_____

_____

_____

_____

Call To Action

_____

30 DAY CHANNEL BUILDER: MISSION COMPLETE !

Now create at least 1 video per week for the rest of the year and you have the foundation of a channel ready for success.

_____

_____

_____

_____

_____

_____

Intro

_____

_____

_____

_____

_____

Story

_____

_____

_____

_____

_____

_____

Call To Action

_____

Intro

Story

Call To Action

Intro

Story

Call To Action

Intro

Story

Call To Action

Intro

Story

Call To Action

Intro

Story

Call To Action

Intro

Story

Call To Action

Intro

Story

Call To Action

_____

_____

_____

_____

_____

Intro

_____

_____

_____

_____

_____

_____

Story

_____

_____

_____

_____

_____

Call To Action

Intro

Story

Call To Action

_____

_____

_____

_____

_____

Intro

_____

_____

_____

_____

Story

_____

_____

_____

_____

Call To Action

_____

Intro

Story

Call To Action

_____

_____

_____

_____

_____

_____

Intro

_____

_____

_____

_____

_____

Story

_____

_____

_____

_____

_____

Call To Action

_____

Intro

Story

Call To Action

_____

_____

_____

_____

_____

Intro

_____

_____

_____

_____

Story

_____

_____

_____

_____

Call To Action

_____

Intro

Story

Call To Action

_____

_____

_____

_____

_____

Intro

_____

_____

_____

_____

Story

_____

_____

_____

_____

Call To Action

_____

Intro

Story

Call To Action

_____

_____

_____

_____

_____

Intro

_____

_____

_____

_____

Story

_____

_____

_____

_____

Call To Action

_____

Intro

Story

Call To Action

_____

_____

_____

_____

_____

Intro

_____

_____

_____

_____

Story

_____

_____

_____

_____

Call To Action

_____

Intro

Story

Call To Action

_____

_____

_____

_____

_____

Intro

_____

_____

_____

_____

Story

_____

_____

_____

_____

Call To Action

_____

Intro

Story

Call To Action

	Intro
	Story
	Call To Action

Intro

Story

Call To Action

Intro

Story

Call To Action

_____

_____

_____

_____

_____

Intro

_____

Story

_____

_____

Call To Action

_____

_____

_____

_____

_____

Intro

Story

Call To Action

_____

_____

_____

_____

_____

Intro

_____

_____

_____

_____

Story

_____

_____

_____

_____

Call To Action

_____

Intro

Story

Call To Action

_____

_____

_____

_____

_____

Intro

_____

_____

_____

_____

Story

_____

_____

_____

_____

Call To Action

_____

Intro

_____
_____
_____
_____
_____
_____

Story

_____
_____
_____
_____
_____
_____

Call To Action

_____
_____
_____
_____
_____
_____

_____

_____

_____

_____

_____

Intro

_____

_____

_____

_____

Story

_____

_____

_____

_____

Call To Action

_____

Intro

Story

Call To Action

_____

_____

_____

_____

Intro

_____

_____

_____

_____

Story

_____

_____

_____

_____

Call To Action

_____

Intro

Story

Call To Action

_____

_____

_____

_____

_____

Intro

_____

_____

_____

_____

Story

_____

_____

_____

_____

Call To Action

_____

Intro

Story

Call To Action

_____

_____

_____

_____

_____

Intro

_____

_____

_____

_____

Story

_____

_____

_____

_____

Call To Action

_____

Intro

Story

Call To Action

_____

_____

_____

_____

_____

_____

Intro

_____

_____

_____

_____

Story

_____

_____

_____

_____

Call To Action

_____

Intro

Story

Call To Action

_____

_____

_____

_____

_____

Intro

_____

_____

_____

_____

Story

_____

_____

_____

_____

Call To Action

_____

Intro

Story

Call To Action

_____

_____

_____

_____

_____

Intro

_____

_____

_____

_____

Story

_____

_____

_____

_____

_____

Call To Action

Intro

Story

Call To Action

THANK YOU FOR YOUR
SUPPORT! I WISH YOU THE
BEST OF LUCK ON YOUR
YOUTUBE RANKING JOURNEY!
IF YOU SHOULD NEED ANY
HELP IN THAT GROWTH JOIN US
IN THE FB GROUP

http://facebook.com/groups/PassiveCashStacker

Made in the USA
Middletown, DE
18 October 2020